T. 1 John
AOR

"This series is a tremendous resource for those wanting [...] understanding of how the gospel is woven throughout Scripture. Here are gospel-minded pastors and scholars doing gospel business from all the Scriptures. This is a biblical and theological feast preparing God's people to apply the entire Bible to all of life with heart and mind wholly committed to Christ's priorities."

> **BRYAN CHAPELL,** President Emeritus, Covenant Theological Seminary; Senior Pastor, Grace Presbyterian Church, Peoria, Illinois

"Mark Twain may have smiled when he wrote to a friend, 'I didn't have time to write you a short letter, so I wrote you a long letter.' But the truth of Twain's remark remains serious and universal, because well-reasoned, compact writing requires extra time and extra hard work. And this is what we have in the Crossway Bible study series *Knowing the Bible*. The skilled authors and notable editors provide the contours of each book of the Bible as well as the grand theological themes that bind them together as one Book. Here, in a 12-week format, are carefully wrought studies that will ignite the mind and the heart."

> **R. KENT HUGHES,** Visiting Professor of Practical Theology, Westminster Theological Seminary

"*Knowing the Bible* brings together a gifted team of Bible teachers to produce a high-quality series of study guides. The coordinated focus of these materials is unique: biblical content, provocative questions, systematic theology, practical application, and the gospel story of God's grace presented all the way through Scripture."

> **PHILIP G. RYKEN,** President, Wheaton College

"These *Knowing the Bible* volumes provide a significant and very welcome variation on the general run of inductive Bible studies. This series provides substantial instruction, as well as teaching through the very questions that are asked. *Knowing the Bible* then goes even further by showing how any given text links with the gospel, the whole Bible, and the formation of theology. I heartily endorse this orientation of individual books to the whole Bible and the gospel, and I applaud the demonstration that sound theology was not something invented later by Christians, but is right there in the pages of Scripture."

> **GRAEME L. GOLDSWORTHY,** former lecturer, Moore Theological College; author, *According to Plan*, *Gospel and Kingdom*, *The Gospel in Revelation*, and *Gospel and Wisdom*

"What a gift to earnest, Bible-loving, Bible-searching believers! The organization and structure of the Bible study format presented through the *Knowing the Bible* series is so well conceived. Students of the Word are led to understand the content of passages through perceptive, guided questions, and they are given rich insights and application all along the way in the brief but illuminating sections that conclude each study. What potential growth in depth and breadth of understanding these studies offer! One can only pray that vast numbers of believers will discover more of God and the beauty of his Word through these rich studies."

> **BRUCE A. WARE,** Professor of Christian Theology, The Southern Baptist Theological Seminary

KNOWING THE BIBLE

J. I. Packer, Theological Editor
Dane C. Ortlund, Series Editor
Lane T. Dennis, Executive Editor

●　　　●　　　●　　　●　　　●　　　●

Genesis	Psalms	Jonah, Micah, and Nahum	Ephesians
Exodus	Proverbs		Philippians
Leviticus	Ecclesiastes	Haggai, Zechariah, and Malachi	Colossians and Philemon
Numbers	Song of Solomon		
Deuteronomy	Isaiah	Matthew	1–2 Thessalonians
Joshua	Jeremiah	Mark	1–2 Timothy and Titus
Judges	Lamentations, Habakkuk, and Zephaniah	Luke	
Ruth and Esther		John	Hebrews
1–2 Samuel		Acts	James
1–2 Kings	Ezekiel	Romans	1–2 Peter and Jude
1–2 Chronicles	Daniel	1 Corinthians	1–3 John
Ezra and Nehemiah	Hosea	2 Corinthians	Revelation
Job	Joel, Amos, and Obadiah	Galatians	

●　　　●　　　●　　　●　　　●　　　●

J. I. PACKER is Board of Governors' Professor of Theology at Regent College (Vancouver, BC). Dr. Packer earned his DPhil at the University of Oxford. He is known and loved worldwide as the author of the best-selling book *Knowing God*, as well as many other titles on theology and the Christian life. He serves as the General Editor of the ESV Bible and as the Theological Editor for the *ESV Study Bible*.

LANE T. DENNIS is President of Crossway, a not-for-profit publishing ministry. Dr. Dennis earned his PhD from Northwestern University. He is Chair of the ESV Bible Translation Oversight Committee and Executive Editor of the *ESV Study Bible*.

DANE C. ORTLUND is Executive Vice President of Bible Publishing and Bible Publisher at Crossway. He is a graduate of Covenant Theological Seminary (MDiv, ThM) and Wheaton College (BA, PhD). Dr. Ortlund has authored several books and scholarly articles in the areas of Bible, theology, and Christian living.

1–3 JOHN

A 12-WEEK STUDY

Michael LeFebvre

WHEATON, ILLINOIS

Cover design: Simplicated Studio

First printing 2018

Printed in the United States of America

Trade paperback ISBN: 978-1-4335-5489-6
EPub ISBN: 978-1-4335-5492-6
PDF ISBN: 978-1-4335-5490-2
Mobipocket ISBN: 978-1-4335-5491-9

Crossway is a publishing ministry of Good News Publishers.

VP			27	26	25	24	23	22	21	20	19	18
15	14	13	12	11	10	9	8	7	6	5	4	3	2	1

TABLE OF CONTENTS

▲

SERIES PREFACE

KNOWING THE BIBLE, as the series title indicates, was created to help readers know and understand the meaning, the message, and the God of the Bible. Each volume in the series consists of 12 units that progressively take the reader through a clear, concise study of one or more books of the Bible. In this way, any given volume can fruitfully be used in a 12-week format either in group study, such as in a church-based context, or in individual study. Of course, these 12 studies could be completed in fewer or more than 12 weeks, as convenient, depending on the context in which they are used.

Each study unit gives an overview of the text at hand before digging into it with a series of questions for reflection or discussion. The unit then concludes by highlighting the gospel of grace in each passage ("Gospel Glimpses"), identifying whole-Bible themes that occur in the passage ("Whole-Bible Connections"), and pinpointing Christian doctrines that are affirmed in the passage ("Theological Soundings").

The final component to each unit is a section for reflecting on personal and practical implications from the passage at hand. The layout provides space for recording responses to the questions proposed, and we think readers need to do this to get the full benefit of the exercise. The series also includes definitions of key words. These definitions are indicated by a note number in the text and are found at the end of each chapter.

Lastly, to help understand the Bible in this deeper way, we urge readers to use the ESV Bible and the *ESV Study Bible*, which are available in various print and digital formats, including online editions at esv.org. The *Knowing the Bible* series is also available online.

May the Lord greatly bless your study as you seek to know him through knowing his Word.

J. I. Packer
Lane T. Dennis

WEEK 1: OVERVIEW

▲

Paul is sometimes called the "apostle of faith." Peter has been called the "apostle of hope." And John has received the attribution of the "apostle of love." All of the apostles taught Christian "faith, hope, and love" (1 Cor. 13:13). Nevertheless, John's epistles are particularly emphatic regarding the Christian calling to love. Out of 221 instances of the word "love" in the New Testament, 42 (or nearly 20 percent) occur in the brief epistles of John. Even though John's epistles are among the shortest books of the Bible, his first letter alone contains more mentions of "love" (36 times) than does any other book in the Bible, save one: only the book of Psalms contains more references to "love." For good reason, these epistles have contributed to John's reputation as the "apostle of love."

But it is not his own message that John writes: "This is the message we have heard from him," that is, from Jesus (1 John 1:5). It is Jesus who has showed us that God is holy, without sin, and abounding in love. Therefore we who have been made children of God through Christ's atoning[1] work ought to cease from sin and grow in love for one another. John writes these three letters to instruct and motivate us in sanctification[2] and love. The motivational character of John's letters is particularly striking. He writes with an emotive, picturesque, rhetorically amplified style designed to stir our hearts as well as instruct our minds.

The three epistles of John form a single "package," probably designed to be taken together. First John is the main document of the three; it is essentially a written sermon and lacks the normal salutation (compare Rom. 1:1–7) and farewell instructions (compare Rom. 16:1–27) of a typical epistle. However, the short letter we know as 2 John contains the elements of a salutation. And 3 John contains the personal instructions often included at the end of an epistle. All three epistles thus probably formed a single packet delivered together: a cover letter to the congregation (2 John), a cover letter to the pastor (3 John), and the main written sermon (1 John). In this study, we will examine the written sermon (1 John) first and then consider the shorter epistles in their likely roles as cover letters. (For further background, see the ESV *Study Bible*, pages 2425–2446; online at esv.org.)

Placing 1–3 John in the Larger Story

Initially, the Scriptures used by the church were those of the Old Testament. Since Jesus came to fulfill all that was promised in the Law and the Prophets (Luke 24:44–45), the church grew in Christian faith through instruction in the Old Testament Scriptures as the apostles[3] testified to their fulfillment in Jesus (Acts 2:14–36; 4:23–31; 7:1–53; 8:26–35; 13:16–41). However, Jewish leaders outside the church (Acts 4:18) as well as some teachers inside the church (Acts 15:5; 1 John 2:18–19) promoted false teachings about the meaning of the Scriptures and the ministry of Jesus. It was urgent to document the apostles' testimony for the wider church and for future generations. Paul (Acts 20:31), Peter (2 Peter 1:15), John, and others of the apostles (1 John 1:3–4) participated in this crucial project of documenting the apostolic testimony concerning Jesus, resulting in the New Testament, which accompanies the Old Testament to form the complete canon of Christian Scripture.

John, who calls himself "the elder" (2 John 1; 3 John 1), was likely the longest-surviving apostle. His epistles are among the final of the apostolic writings provided to secure the church in the "message we have heard from him" (1 John 1:5) in the face of false teachers (1 John 2:18–26).

Key Verses

"Do not love the world or the things in the world. If anyone loves the world, the love of the Father is not in him. . . . The world is passing away along with its desires, but whoever does the will of God abides forever." (1 John 2:15–17)

Date and Historical Background

After Christ's ascension, John continued to minister in Jerusalem alongside the other apostles (Acts 8:1). Early church fathers indicate that he left Jerusalem just prior to the Roman destruction of the city in AD 70. John reportedly spent his later years in Ephesus, until his exile to the Isle of Patmos (Rev. 1:9). Most scholars believe that John wrote his eponymous epistles while laboring in Ephesus. If this is correct, he likely wrote these letters to other churches in the vicinity of Ephesus (see Rev. 2:8–3:22). Alternatively, if John wrote these letters toward the end of his years in Jerusalem, he may have addressed them to the church in Ephesus itself while already anticipating a move there (2 John 12; 3 John 10, 13).

Outline

1 John: The Written Sermon

I. Introduction (1:1–2:14)

   A. John's authority (1:1–4)

   B. John's message (1:5–10)

   C. John's reason for writing (2:1–14)

II. Main Exhortation: Love the Father, Not the World (2:15–17)

III. Lessons on Christian Faithfulness (2:18–5:12)

   A. Beware of antichrists (2:18–27)

   B. Abide in Christ (2:28–3:10)

   C. Love one another in truth, taught by God's Spirit (3:11–4:6)

   D. Love one another as God has loved us (4:7–21)

   E. Victory and life come through Christ (5:1–12)

IV. Conclusion: Know That You Have Eternal Life (5:13–21)

2 John: Cover Letter to the Congregation

V. Salutation to the Congregation (vv. 1–3)

VI. Synopsis of the "Written Sermon" (vv. 4–11)

   A. Walk in the truth (vv. 4–6)

   B. Abstain from error (vv. 7–11)

VII. Farewell (vv. 12–13)

3 John: Cover Letter to the Pastor

VIII. Salutation to Gaius (v. 1)

IX. Personal Instructions (vv. 2–12)

A. Instructions for Gaius (vv. 2–8)

B. Instructions regarding Diotrephes (vv. 9–10)

C. Instructions regarding Demetrius (vv. 11–12)

X. Farewell (vv. 13–15)

As You Get Started

The apostle John is mentioned 30 times in the books of Matthew, Mark, Luke, Acts, and Galatians. John also features as a character in his own Gospel and throughout the book of Revelation, which is also traditionally attributed to him. What do you know about John, his life, and his personality, from previous study of the New Testament?

He died of natural causes.

Apart from Paul, John was probably the most prolific writer among the apostles. He left us a Gospel, three epistles, and the book of Revelation. Which of these have you read or heard sermons about? What general themes or impressions do you associate with John's writings?

Gospel. He emphasized the deity of Christ and the essentials of salvation.

Of the 12 disciples, John was one of the three (along with his brother James and Peter) who were closest to Jesus and spent the most intimate time with him (see Mark 5:37; 9:2; 14:33). John was also the disciple sitting closest to Jesus at the Last Supper (John 13:23–25), the only one of the Twelve who was present at the crucifixion, and the one to whom Jesus entrusted the care of and for his mother, Mary (John 19:26–27). If you could ask John one or two questions about his experience with Jesus, what would you ask him? What do you hope to learn from him in these three epistles?

How do you substantiate many of the claims? What exactly is being implied? What did you do to ensure your writings would be recorded accurately?

As You Finish This Unit . . .

Give thanks to God that he inspired the apostle John to leave us these precious instructions concerning Christ, whom he knew and whom he helps us to know as well. Pray for God's Spirit to open your heart to grow in your love for Christ as you learn about him from John's letters.

Definitions

[1] **Atonement** – The reconciliation of a person with God, often associated with the offering of a sacrifice. Through his death and resurrection, Jesus Christ made atonement for the sins of believers. His death satisfied God's just wrath against sinful humanity, just as OT sacrifices symbolized substitutionary death as payment for sin.

[2] **Sanctification** – The process of being conformed to the image of Jesus Christ through the work of the Holy Spirit. This process begins immediately after regeneration and continues throughout a Christian's life.

[3] **Apostle** – Means "one who is sent" and refers to one who is an official representative of another. In the NT, refers specifically to those whom Jesus chose to represent him.

WEEK 2: THIS IS THE MESSAGE

1 John 1:1–2:11

The Place of the Passage

First John opens with an introduction to the writer's authority (1:1–4), his message (1:5–10), and his reason for writing (2:1–14). John's authority to declare the message of Jesus is grounded in his own in-person fellowship with the Lord. With vivid imagery, John leads us to reimagine our own church[1] assemblies as participating in those gatherings of Jesus with his apostles. The message of John's letter is that which he heard from Jesus in those gatherings. Jesus taught the holiness of God and the cleansing that he himself provides for our communion with the Lord. It is John's reason for writing that constitutes the longest part of this introduction. He writes to press Christians with the implications of that message from Jesus, namely, to cease from sin and to love one another.

The Big Picture

Jesus forgives sinners so that they can cease from sin and grow in love.

> ## Reflection and Discussion

This passage is divided into three sections below. Skim the whole passage quickly and then read each section slowly before interacting with the questions under each heading. (Further insight is available in the notes on pages 2430–2431 of the *ESV Study Bible*, also available at esv.org.)

1. John's Authority: Being with Jesus (1:1–4)

John is an encourager. He writes in a manner that stirs our imagination as he speaks about Jesus. List below the different physical senses John evokes as he recalls the disciples' in-person experiences of Christ.

Sight, Touch, hearing

John twice uses the term "fellowship" to describe our relationships with Christ, with the Father through Christ, and with one another in his church. How does John's description challenge us to refresh our vision of the church's gatherings?

community, do we

Compare the beginning of John's epistle with the beginning of his Gospel (John 1:1–18). List parallels that you note.

Christs sacrifice, unity an life

2. John's Message: Retelling the Gospel (1:5–10)

John exposes three incorrect methods that some use in trying to qualify for fellowship with God. What are these three false bases for fellowship with God that John rejects (see the three "if we say" statements in vv. 6, 8, and 10)?

live according to truth, Bragging

In between these three false claims, John weaves two marks of those who are accepted by God. What are these marks of genuine fellowship with God (see the "if we walk" and "if we confess" phrases in vv. 7 and 9)?

in the light, we have sinned.

Both marks of those in God's fellowship end with the same glorious promise. What is this promise for those who "walk" and "confess" in the way John describes (vv. 7b and 9b)? How does this promise enable our fellowship with the God of "light," in whom there is "no darkness" (v. 5)?

forgiveness, purify

3. John's Purpose: Renewing Fellowship (2:1–11)

Next, the apostle presents two purpose statements for his letter, each introduced with a word of address: "My little children, I am writing . . ." (vv. 1–6) and

"Beloved, I am writing . . ." (vv. 7–11). In your own words, summarize the first purpose John gives for writing this letter (vv. 1–6).

avoid sin

John's first purpose statement addresses sin and forgiveness, but his second purpose statement (vv. 7–11) concerns love. In addition to renewed communion with God, with whom else is our fellowship restored by the gospel?

Remind of old command

John compares the "old commandment" to love with the "new commandment" he heard from Jesus. Compare the Old Testament love commandment in Leviticus 19:18 with the new commandment from Jesus in John 13:34. What remains the same, and what is different?

Love

Read through the following three sections on *Gospel Glimpses*, *Whole-Bible Connections*, and *Theological Soundings*. Then take time to consider the *Personal Implications* these sections may have for you.

Gospel Glimpses

PROPITIATION. John identifies Jesus as both our "advocate with the Father" (2:1) and the "propitiation for our sins" (2:2). The title "advocate" points to the role Jesus undertakes to intercede on our behalf before the court of heaven. The title "propitiation" points to his becoming, by his sacrifice on the cross, the payment required to satisfy the damages caused by our sins and to quench the just wrath of God aroused by those sins. The word "propitiation" comes from the Latin word for "favor" (compare the English word "propitious"). Our sins justly deserve God's wrath, but Jesus' sacrifice provided the payment to satisfy heaven's justice. With God's wrath satisfied, the sacrifice of Jesus is said to "propitiate" or restore favor with God.

HOLINESS. Christians sometimes focus on the joy of forgiveness and neglect the other side of the gospel: renewal in holiness.[2] John reminds us that the marvel of the gospel is that Jesus both forgives our sins and leads us into new holiness. He writes that the sum of God's holy commands is love (2:7–11; compare Matt. 22:37–40; Gal. 5:14). To be restored to holiness is to be renewed to a life of love for God and for one another. Sin breaks relationships. The gospel cleanses us from sin and renews us in holy love.

Whole-Bible Connections

IN THE BEGINNING. John is a serious student of the book of Genesis. He repeatedly references Genesis as he draws lessons and doctrines "from the beginning" (1 John 1:1; 2:7, 13, 14, 24; 3:8, 11; 2 John 5, 6; see also John 1:1, 2; 8:44; Rev. 3:14; 21:6; 22:13). Genesis 1:1 starts, "In the beginning," and uses the same term (*archē*) in the Septuagint (LXX; the Greek translation of the Old Testament) that John uses in his references to that verse. In this week's passage, John tells us that the man Jesus is more than a mere man. He is one and the same with "the word of life" (1 John 1:1; compare John 1:1) who brought the world into existence. John further points to Genesis when he identifies the love commandment as a commandment that we have had "from the beginning" (1 John 2:7); when he refers to the lesson of Cain and Abel (3:11–12; compare Gen. 4:1–16); and when he mentions the "devil" as the serpent who introduced sin "from the beginning" (1 John 3:8; compare John 8:44; Rev. 12:9; 20:2).

WRITING APOSTLES. The ministry of the apostles was primarily a work of in-person preaching, shepherding, and church planting. Through live proclamation, the apostles related the events and teachings of Jesus over and over. But as they approached the end of their lives, it was important to ensure that their testimony to the works of Jesus would continue. Whatever writing the apostles may have done early in their ministries, there are also references throughout the New Testament to the special urgency to write things down toward the end of their lives. Peter expresses this motivation for his writing (2 Pet. 1:12–15). John tells us that he and other apostles are doing the same (1 John 1:3–4).

Theological Soundings

FELLOWSHIP. John tends to use descriptive terms in his epistles in order to evoke richer experiences of the things he describes. One example of this is his word choice for describing the church in 1:3–4, 6–7. John describes the church as the assembly of those who hear and believe the testimony of the apostles. He uses the term "fellowship" (four times!) to describe these assemblies rather than the normal term "church." The Greek word is *koinōnia*, and it refers to more than casual friendship. The Greek term indicates a partnership in which each member takes a stake in the success of the whole. (The J. R. R. Tolkien novel *The Fellowship of the Ring* is a good illustration of this concept of a "fellowship.") John uses this term to describe the nature of the church as a society whose members have mutual duties to one another.

SIN. When facing a court deposition, as an inquiring attorney is seeking evidence to condemn, it is natural for a defendant to hide as much as possible. But when talking with a doctor, whose inquiries are made in order to heal, a patient wants to bring every possible symptom and test result into the light. Similarly, John teaches us not to be afraid to acknowledge and confess our sins. Repentance[3] and the resulting forgiveness are beautifully expressed in 1 John. Furthermore, John teaches us something fascinating about the nature of sin: after condemning sin in 2:1–6, John proceeds to show us the opposite of sin in verses 7–11. That opposite is "love." Once we understand this, we ought to yearn all the more to face our sins and repent of them, replacing them with genuine love for one another and for God.

Personal Implications

As you reflect on John's introductory lessons on the church, the gospel, and the beauty of Christian love, consider their relevance to your own life today. Write down your reflections under the three headings we have considered and on the passage as a whole.

1. Gospel Glimpses

2. Whole-Bible Connections

3. Theological Soundings

4. 1 John 1:1–2:11

As You Finish This Unit . . .

Be sure to conclude your study of these passages with prayer. Ask the Spirit to search your heart, to grant you grace to repent of abiding sins, and to fill you with increasing love for your brothers and sisters in the church.

Definitions

[1] **Church** – From a Greek word meaning "assembly." The body of believers in Jesus Christ, referring either to all believers everywhere or to a local gathering of believers.

[2] **Holiness** – A quality possessed by something or someone set apart for special use. When applied to God, it refers to his utter perfection and complete transcendence over creation. God's people are called to imitate his holiness (Lev. 19:2), which means being set apart from sin and reserved for God's purposes.

[3] **Repentance** – A complete change of heart and mind regarding one's overall attitude toward God or one's individual actions. True regeneration and conversion is always accompanied by repentance.

WEEK 3: DO NOT LOVE THE WORLD

1 John 2:12–17

▲

> ## The Place of the Passage

In the previous section (1 John 1:1–2:11), John introduced his authority for writing this epistle, the message of the epistle, and his purpose in writing it. In 2:12–14, John's introduction of his reason for writing continues with a poetic address to each of the various groups within his audience. Then, having introduced the letter and his reasons for writing, John declares the primary exhortation of the book (2:15–17). In New Testament times, sermons and speeches typically began with an introduction (an *exordium*) followed by the speaker's primary exhortation (the *propositio*). John delivers the main exhortation of his epistle (the *propositio*) in 2:15–17. This is where we learn what the apostle expects of his audience in response to the message he is delivering in this letter.

> ## The Big Picture

Being forgiven and enrolled into the fellowship of heaven, Christians must cease loving the world[1] and its sins.

> ## Reflection and Discussion

Quickly review the previous section, the beginning of the epistle's introduction (1:1–2:11). Then carefully read the poetic climax of that introduction in 2:12–14. Respond to the discussion questions for verses 12–14 below, then read and interact with the questions regarding the epistle's proposition statement in verses 15–17. (See also pages 2431–2432 of the *ESV Study Bible*, also available online at esv.org.)

1. Motivating to Listen (2:12–14)

John addresses three groups: "little children," "fathers," and "young men." Commentators debate whether these groups represent physical ages or stages of spiritual maturity. Considering the content of each address, what is your sense of whom these terms represent, and why?

John urges Christians to build on the strengths they already possess at their current stages in life. Summarize in your own words one key spiritual strength John emphasizes for each group.

a. "little children" (vv. 12a, 13c):

b. "fathers" (vv. 13a, 14a):

c. "young men" (vv. 13b, 14b):

John adopts the pen of a poet in these verses, using succinct, versified phrases and also repetition. Some scholars think his switch in tenses is likewise based on poetic technique. Three phrases employ the present tense, "I am writing." The three phrases are then repeated in the past tense: "I wrote" (some translations use "I write," but this verb form is normally past tense). Poetically, this juxtaposition of tenses turns the epistle into a "bridge" between the author's time and place (for whom the letter is *being* written: "I am writing") and that of the reader (for whom John's letter is *finished*: what he "wrote"). How does this effort to create a poetic bridge between the author's time and that of the recipients relate to John's purposes in 1:3–4?

John's groupings jump from youngest to eldest and then end each time with the middle group. This indicates John's particular focus on youth. In the first address to the youth of the church, John commends their victory over temptation (v. 13b). In his second address to them, he makes an important addition. What does John identify as the basis whereby young people are enabled to continue in victory (v. 14b)?

2. Exhorting to Respond (2:15–17)

In verses 15–17, John states our expected response to the message of Jesus: we are to love the Father and not to love the world (compare 2:1). What are the marks of one who loves the world?

What are the marks of one who loves the Father?

In verse 16, John lists two "desires" ("desires of the flesh and . . . of the eyes")
and one attitude ("pride in possessions"; ESV footnote) that we ought not have
toward the "things in the world." It is not the *things* in the world but the *love*
of those things that is inherently sinful. List a couple of specific examples of
modern sins belonging to each category ("desires of the flesh," "desires of the
eyes," "pride in possessions").

What does John say about the world and its desires that helps us to see how
abstaining from these sins is not loss but is for our ultimate gain?

These verses introduce the main exhortation of John's epistle (vv. 15–17). Peek
ahead to the command in 1 John 5:21 that ends the epistle. How do these opening and closing commands relate?

Read through the following three sections on *Gospel Glimpses, Whole-Bible Connections*, and *Theological Soundings*. Then take time to consider the *Personal Implications* these sections may have for you.

Gospel Glimpses

SAVED FOR RELATIONSHIP. In John's poetic address in 2:12–14, he breaks down the experience of salvation[2] into three parts. To the "children," John speaks of the joy of forgiveness through Christ (v. 12) and of a new relationship with the Father (v. 13c). To the "young men," John speaks of sanctification and victory over sin (vv. 13b, 14b). To the "fathers," he writes about their communion with the same Lord who has been at work among his people "from the beginning" (vv. 13a, 14a). Notably, it is the believer's right relationship with God that provides both the beginning foundation (v. 13c) and the mature reward (vv. 13a, 14a) of our salvation.

JUDGMENT. Judgment is not always bad. When a judge renders a verdict, that judgment brings punishment to the guilty but it also brings reward to the vindicated. In the Bible, God's judgment is something that the innocent and the oppressed long for (see Pss. 7:8–11; 72:1–4) but that the unrepentant wicked ought to dread. At the heart of the gospel is the Christian's hope and longing for the final judgment, when those whose sins have been forgiven will enter their eternal inheritance and the sins of the world will be purged forever. In 1 John 2:15–17, John teaches us to view the world and its sins through these "gospel judgment" lenses.

Whole-Bible Connections

PASSING WORLD. Ever since the Lord pronounced a curse when Adam and Eve ate from the forbidden tree (Gen. 2:17), and Noah preached of a coming flood upon the world of his day (Genesis 6–9), God's prophets have warned both of imminent judgments and of a future, final judgment upon the world. From Genesis to Revelation, the Bible is full of warnings concerning the "passing away" of the present world order and its sins. John contributes to this meta-theme of the Bible in 1 John 2:16–17.

Theological Soundings

SIN. In this week's passage, John teaches much about the nature of sin and our battle against it. Even Christians who are in a living relationship with the Lord will still experience temptation. Our forgiveness is complete at the cross of Christ (v. 12), but our struggle against sin is not complete until "the world pass[es] away along with its desires" (v. 17). Nevertheless, building God's Word and its truths into our hearts gives us strength to resist sin (v. 14) and to grow in our love for the Father and for one another.

FAITH AND WORKS. John helps us see the proper relationship between faith and works in the Christian life. It is by faith alone that the believer is forgiven and adopted into the family of God. Nevertheless, if that faith is genuine, then works of godly love and holiness will necessarily follow. Electricity is not created in a circuit by the shining of the light bulb attached to it; nevertheless, a connected, intact light bulb will begin to shine once the electricity is flowing. Similarly, John points us to faith as the power of our salvation, and to works of love for others as the necessary result and thus the tangible indicator of new life within.

Personal Implications

John writes to us with words of life and victory over sin. These are truths for us to live by, and not just to think about. Make notes below on some personal implications for your walk with the Lord under the three headings we have considered and on the passage as a whole.

1. Gospel Glimpses

2. Whole-Bible Connections

3. Theological Soundings

---

4. 1 John 2:12–17

As You Finish This Unit . . .

There is a reason why John felt compelled to write to the church with these exhortations. The temptations of the world still pull strongly upon us, and we need these encouragements to turn away from sin (self-love) and to nurture holiness (love for God and others) in our hearts instead. Pray for the Holy Spirit to use the Scriptures (including this study!) to strengthen your heart in victory over sin.

Definitions

[1] **World** – In Scripture, the context determines the meaning of this term. The physical world is God's creation of the earth and everything in it. It can refer to all of humanity (John 3:16) or to the unbelieving, godless world system (John 1:10)—often as an adjective: "worldly" (1 Cor. 1:26).

[2] **Salvation** – Deliverance from the eternal consequences of sin. Jesus' death and resurrection purchased eternal salvation for believers (Rom. 1:16).

WEEK 4: ABIDE IN HIM

1 John 2:18–3:10

▲

In the previous two weeks, we studied the introductory parts of John's letter. The introduction (1 John 1:1–2:14) was capped off with John's main exhortation (the *propositio* section; 2:15–17), in which he called his readers to love the Father and to reject the sins of the world. We now begin a series of lessons that constitute the body of John's epistle and flesh out the truths identified in the introduction and main exhortation. The first two lessons, which we will consider in this week's study, are each introduced by the direct address "children" or "little children" (2:18, 28). In the first lesson (2:18–27), John teaches the Christ-centered nature of genuine faith. In order to know the Father, we must confess the Son, as the Spirit uses the Scriptures to teach about him. In the second lesson (2:28–3:10), John teaches the fruit of genuine Christian faith, which is righteousness that produces love.

The Big Picture

Being born anew through Christ, Christians will grow in God's likeness, just as children mature into the likeness of their parents.

> ## Reflection and Discussion

Read each section indicated below, one at a time. Stop after each reading to reflect on the passage using the provided questions. Write your answers along with other insights. (For notes to help further stimulate your own thoughts on the passage, consult the *ESV Study Bible*, pages 2432–2433, also online at esv.org.)

1. The Triune Love of God (2:18–27)

John writes to a church that has recently experienced turmoil. False teachers who denied that Jesus is the Son of God had emerged within the congregation (vv. 22–23). They eventually left the church, leading others out with them (v. 19). John writes to affirm those who have remained faithful to Christ. What title does John give for the false teachers, and what does this title mean (vv. 18, 22)?

John alternates between the errors of the false teachers (vv. 18–19, 22–23) and his words of assurance to the faithful (vv. 20–21, 24–25). What are some of the marks of those whose teaching is not true? What are the sources of assurance John mentions concerning what is true about Jesus?

John points to each person of the Trinity as fulfilling a role in our faith. He also identifies the role of Scripture ("what you heard from the beginning"; v. 24) in the life of the church. What roles of the Scriptures and of each person of the Trinity are identified by John?

a. The Father:

b. Jesus Christ, the Son:

c. The Spirit, the Holy One:

d. Scripture ("what you heard from the beginning"):

In light of the letter's original context—a church divided by false teachers, who are opposed by those who have remained faithful to "what you heard from the beginning" (v. 24)—what does the apostle mean when he says, "You have no need that anyone should teach you" (v. 27)?

2. Children of God (2:28–3:10)

A teacher shows love when he instructs his students; a doctor shows love when she treats the unwell; many different roles illustrate love. What kind of role does

John use to express God's love? Why is God's love for us such a cause of wonder ("See what kind of love"; 3:1)?

On the one hand, John likens Christians to adopted children: the phrase "called children of God" (3:1) is the language of adoption. On the other hand, John describes us as God's biological offspring (v. 9). How does each of these images illustrate important features of the Christian life?

If we are not growing in the likeness of Christ, to whose image does John warn us we might be conforming ourselves (v. 8)?

Throughout this week's passage, John has exhorted his readers to pursue the righteousness of Christ. In the final verse of the passage, what does John emphasize as the chief expression of that righteousness (v. 10)?

Read through the following three sections on *Gospel Glimpses, Whole-Bible Connections,* and *Theological Soundings.* Then take time to consider the *Personal Implications* these sections may have for you.

Gospel Glimpses

ABIDING. Eight times in this passage, John speaks of our "abiding" in the Lord. In doing so he echoes the language of his Savior (John 15:1–17). The term "abide" captures the relational character of our status as well as the steadfastness of that position. The gospel brings us into a standing of peace with God that is free from any fear of being abandoned by him.

CHILDREN OF GOD. John invokes the language both of adoption and of biological birth. Each provides a different insight into the character of our salvation. The language of adoption reminds us that God has loved us so much that he chose to make us his own, even though he had no obligation to do so. The metaphor of biological offspring captures the intention of God to nurture us into his own likeness, as biological offspring bear the "seed" (in modern terminology, the DNA) of their parents. Neither image is sufficient in itself to capture the greatness of the gospel, but together they paint a glorious picture of the Lord's posture toward us.

Whole-Bible Connections

RESISTANCE TO THE APOSTLES. Jesus taught thousands of disciples, but he specially commissioned 12 to be his apostles (Luke 6:13–16). The apostles received authority to form the New Testament church and to resolve questions about the teachings of Jesus (see 1 John 1:1–4). But not everyone accepted the apostles' authority. For example, some rejected the apostles' teaching that the cross rendered the temple rituals "obsolete" (Heb. 8:13; compare Gal. 3:1–14). Early in the Jerusalem church, some "believers who belonged to the party of the Pharisees rose up and said, 'It is necessary to circumcise[1] [Gentile converts] and to order them to keep the law of Moses'" (Acts 15:5). Paul and the other apostles, as those personally commissioned by Jesus, labored against such false teachers (Gal. 2:11–14). John confronts a similar phenomenon in these letters. Teachers within the church have defied the apostles' teaching (1 John 2:19; compare 3 John 9) that Jesus is the Christ (hence their designation as "antichrist"). They still believe in the God of Israel, but they deny the apostolic confession concerning Jesus as the Messiah. John writes to show that "No one who denies the Son has the Father" (1 John 2:23; compare John 14:6). Like vigilant shepherds, the apostles labored to conserve the church according to the command of Jesus (2 John 8).

Theological Soundings

ANTICHRIST. Among all of the New Testament writers, only John uses the term "antichrist." In each instance of its use (1 John 2:18, 22; 4:3; 2 John 7), John applies the designation to opponents in his own day who deny Christ. Nevertheless, John speaks of these "antichrists" as the fulfillment of previous prophetic warnings and a mark of the "last hour" (1 John 2:18). Some Christians recognize harmonies between John's depictions of the "spirit of the antichrist" (4:3) and Paul's discussion of a singular "man of lawlessness" who must appear prior to the return of Jesus (2 Thess. 2:3–12). Consequently, the title "antichrist" has been identified in many church traditions with an eschatological embodiment of evil expected at the end of history. John's primary use of the title, however, is simply as a *category* of false teachers that has troubled the church ever since the first century.

HOLY SPIRIT. False teachers had unsettled the congregation to whom John wrote. It might be inferred from the text (1 John 2:18–27) that these "antichrists" had overwhelmed the other believers with their learning and ability to cite (and misuse) the Scriptures. To reassure the remnant, John offers a robust doctrine of the Holy Spirit. It is ultimately the Spirit who stirs understanding and conviction. Human teachers are a normal tool of the Spirit in the church (Eph. 4:11–16). Ultimately, however, the Christian leans on the authority of Scripture under the conviction of God's Spirit. "Let what you heard from the beginning abide in you" (1 John 2:24), John urges, referring to the Scriptures from Genesis onward. The teaching of the Spirit is not something Christians receive mystically, apart from Scripture. Nevertheless, the Spirit is himself the believer's ultimate Teacher. While teachers are a normal part of the church, "You have no need that anyone should teach you" (2:27). This is not a word of permission to ignore pastors and teachers (Heb. 13:7, 17). Rather, it is a word of assurance, especially when false teachers spread confusion, that Christians can depend on the Spirit's guidance as they examine the Scriptures.

TRINITY. Of all the New Testament authors, John is the most expansive in his teaching concerning the triune nature of the Godhead. He alone reports the detail of Jesus' "Upper Room Discourse," wherein Jesus teaches the disciples about relations within the triune Godhead (John 13–17). The three persons of the Trinity also receive attention throughout John's epistles, including in this week's passage. In 1 John 2:18–27, John encourages the faithful remnant by affirming their relationship with the Father, through the mediation of the Son, and by the conviction and instruction of the Spirit.

Personal Implications

As you reflect on the lessons John gave us in this week's study, record points of personal application. Make notes below on some personal implications for your walk with the Lord under the three headings we have considered and on the passage as a whole.

1. Gospel Glimpses

2. Whole-Bible Connections

3. Theological Soundings

4. 1 John 2:18–3:10

As You Finish This Unit . . .

As you close in prayer, give thanks to each person of the Godhead. Give thanks to the Father for having loved you enough to choose you as his child. Give thanks to the Son for having accomplished our atonement for us. And give thanks to the Spirit for daily sustaining your faith through the Scriptures.

Definition

[1] **Circumcision** – The ritual practice of removing the foreskin of an individual, which was commanded for all male Israelites in OT times as a sign of participation in the covenant God established with Abraham (Gen. 17:9–14).

WEEK 5: LOVE ONE ANOTHER

1 John 3:11–4:6

▲

John's next lesson unfolds along a series of three "by this we know" themes: (1) "by this we know love" (3:16); (2) "by this we shall know . . . that we are of the truth" (3:19); and (3) "by this you know the Spirit of God" (4:2, 6). These are not three separate topics; they are interdependent parts of a single lesson. This can be seen by looking at the construction of the passage. Last week's reading ended with a reference to "love" as the key manifestation of righteousness (3:10), a reference that also introduces the first "by this we know" section in this week's reading: "by this we know love" (3:11–15). These instructions on love end with the need for love's grounding in "truth" (v. 18), which leads to the next point: "by this we . . . know . . . truth" (vv. 19–24). And this discussion of truth ends with our dependence on the "Spirit whom he has given us" (v. 24) for discerning truth, which in turn leads to the section on "know[ing] the Spirit of God" (4:1–6) and distinguishing his work from false spirits. Thus the main theme of this lesson is "love," a love that must be grounded in truth as taught by God's Spirit.

The Big Picture

The Spirit of God convicts and comforts us in the truth in order to produce Christlike love in our lives.

Reflection and Discussion

Read each of the three "by this we know" stages of this lesson on love, pausing after each reading to answer the provided questions. (If you have the *ESV Study Bible*, have pages 2434–2435 open to reference the notes provided there, or access the same notes online at esv.org.)

1. By This We Know Love (3:11–18)

John introduces the nature of love with two examples: Cain (vv. 11–12; compare Gen. 4:1–8) and Jesus (1 John 3:16). How does Cain's lack of love contrast with Jesus' perfect love?

The stakes are life and death in both of John's examples: Cain, in his wickedness, killed his brother, whereas Jesus, out of his love, gave his life for us. Such drastic examples make John's lesson clear: love requires sacrifice. But one does not have to die in order to show love. How ought we to sacrifice in order to show Christlike love (vv. 17–18)?

2. By This We Know Truth (3:19–24)

Our deeds of love must be deeds of *true* love. The phrase "in deed and in truth" means "in deeds—in true ones!" (v. 18). It is God's commandments that teach us true love (3:24; Gal. 5:14), by both convicting us (1 John 3:20) and comforting us (v. 21). What two kinds of responses does John encourage in light of the convictions and comforts of God's commandments (vv. 22–23)?

The commandments of God are numerous. But John summarizes all of God's commandments into two commands (v. 23). What are they? How do these two commands summarize the rest?

3. By This We Know the Spirit (4:1–6)

It is God's Spirit who convicts and comforts us in the truth (3:19–24). Therefore, "testing the spirits" is vital to ensuring that we are being convicted rightly (4:1–6). The Spirit himself is beyond our testing, but John tells us how to discern which *human* teachers are of the "Spirit of God" (v. 2) and which are of the "spirit of the antichrist" (v. 3). A minister of God's Spirit is one who "confesses that Jesus Christ has come in the flesh" (v. 2). This probably means more than simply stating the basic fact of the incarnation; it likely refers to rightly confessing all that was true of Jesus while he was here on earth. In other words, a Spirit-led teacher is identifiable by his consistency with the apostles' testimony of Jesus' earthly life in the flesh (v. 6). If this interpretation is correct, what identifies those teachers who promote a false spirit of antichrist (v. 3)?

Certain false teachers sought to draw believers back to the Jewish temple and away from full confidence in Christ as our final sacrifice (Gal. 1:6–9). The witness of the apostles who heard, saw, and touched Jesus (1 John 1:2–3) is therefore foundational to our faith. In this light, why is John's bold statement in verse 6 so important?

John's exhortation reaches a climax with a threefold emphasis on "listening" (4:5–6). What are some of the "voices" in our society that seek to shape us, and how can we ensure that it is the teaching of the apostles that shapes us instead?

Read through the following three sections on *Gospel Glimpses*, *Whole-Bible Connections*, and *Theological Soundings*. Then take time to consider the *Personal Implications* these sections may have for you.

Gospel Glimpses

THE CROSS. When John speaks about love, he can point to no greater example than the cross of Jesus Christ. "By this we know love," he writes, "that [Jesus] laid down his life for us" (1 John 3:16). May we never grow weary of pondering the majesty of the gospel, that God our Creator loved us enough to send his own Son to die for us! And what a marvel that the Son also loved us so much that he willingly laid down his life for us!

BELIEVE. Normally in Scripture, when God's law[1] is summarized in two points, the two summary commands are these: "You shall love the Lord your God . . . , and your neighbor as yourself" (Luke 10:27). In this week's passage, John condenses the commandments of God to these: "Believe in the name of his Son Jesus Christ and love one another" (1 John 3:23). This is actually saying the same thing as Christ's summary in Luke 10, but John emphasizes the need for faith in Jesus as the centerpiece of our love for the Lord. The gospel is a commandment from God, but it is a commandment that renews us in the love of God.

Whole-Bible Connections

CAIN. John expects his audience to be familiar with the narrative of Cain, who killed his brother Abel. The story is recorded in Genesis 4:1–16. At the heart of this narrative is the question Cain asks when God confronts him concerning the death of Abel. Cain asks, "Am I my brother's keeper?" (Gen. 4:9). The implication of the passage is that, yes, we are each duty-bound to guard the welfare of others, which is precisely how John applies the story of Cain in this letter.

GOOD WORKS. All through the New Testament, apostles repeat the consistent message that Christians must love others actively. Paul writes, "As we have opportunity, let us do good to everyone, and especially to those who are of the household of faith" (Gal. 6:10). He also writes that "we are . . . created in Christ Jesus for good works, which God prepared beforehand, that we should walk in them" (Eph. 2:10). The apostle James challenges, "If a brother or sister is poorly clothed and lacking in daily food, and one of you says to them, 'Go in peace, be warmed and filled,' without giving them the things needed for the body, what good is that? So also faith by itself, if it does not have works, is dead" (James 2:15–17). Good works are not what save us, but deeds of love are the evidence of a living faith[2] within us.

> ## Theological Soundings

EXAMPLE. An orthodox[3] theology of the cross recognizes that Jesus died as a substitute. He was a sacrificial lamb who took upon himself the wrath of God in order that those who trust in him might not suffer God's wrath but rather might share in the inheritance Jesus earned for us (1 John 2:2; compare Isa. 53:4–5; Rom. 4:25; 1 Cor. 15:3; 2 Cor. 5:21). We call this doctrine "substitutionary atonement." Sometimes, theologians have challenged this doctrine by saying that Jesus' obedience to the point of death was merely to teach *us* obedience. It is incorrect to say that Jesus' death was only a moral example and thereby deny its central function as substitutionary atonement. Nevertheless, the apostle John—who himself describes Christ's death as a substitutionary "propitiation" for our sins (1 John 2:2; 4:10)—tells us that Jesus' death should also serve as an example by which we learn to love (3:16). None of us can imitate Christ and be an atoning sacrifice for others; his sacrifice is unrepeatable. Nevertheless, the love through which he atoned for us should impress us to sacrifice also in love for our neighbors.

CONVICTION. John teaches us to welcome God's conviction (1 John 3:20). A sense of guilt for sin is unpleasant (see Psalm 38), but it is not to be resisted. John points to the experience of conviction as a basis for assurance that we are growing in the truth. For "whenever our heart condemns us," we take comfort in the knowledge that God is the one who examines us and stirs that conviction for our good.

Personal Implications

John's lessons on love, truth, and heeding the ministry of the Spirit are addressed to us for our own application. Make notes below on some personal implications for your walk with the Lord under the three headings we have considered and on the passage as a whole.

1. Gospel Glimpses

2. Whole-Bible Connections

3. Theological Soundings

4. 1 John 3:11–4:6

As You Finish This Unit . . .

As you come to the end of this study, thank God in prayer for the gifts of his Spirit and his Word that both teach and convict us in the way of love.

Definitions

[1] **Law** – When spelled with an initial capital letter, "Law" refers to the first five books of the Bible. The Law contains numerous commands of God to his people, including the Ten Commandments and instructions regarding worship, sacrifice, and life in Israel. The NT often uses "the law" (lower case) to refer to the entire body of precepts set forth in the books of the Law.

[2] **Faith** – Trust in or reliance upon something or someone despite a lack of concrete proof. Salvation, which is purely a work of God's grace, can be received only through faith (Rom. 5:2; Eph. 2:8–9). The writer of Hebrews calls on believers to emulate those who lived godly lives by faith (Hebrews 11).

[3] **Orthodoxy** – Teaching and doctrine regarded as correct and in agreement with essential biblical teachings.

WEEK 6: LOVE ONE ANOTHER, CONTINUED

1 John 4:7–21

▲

The Place of the Passage

Last week's passage began by declaring, "We should love one another" (3:11). This week's passage resumes the same instruction: "Beloved, let us love one another" (4:7). Throughout this next set of teachings on love, John uses repetition to overwhelm us with the love of God for us. John does so in order to stir up our love for the Lord in response. But "no one has ever seen God" (4:12, 20). How, then, can we show our love for God in response to his great love for us? John's answer to this dilemma is powerful: "If we love one another, . . . his love is perfected in us" (4:12). The way we show our love for God is by our sacrificial love for one another: "Whoever loves God must also love his brother" (4:21).

The Big Picture

The way in which Christians show love for God is by loving one another.

> **Reflection and Discussion**

The thoughts in this passage are lofty, featuring emphatic, recurring ideas. Read each section slowly and thoughtfully—at least two times each, if possible—before interacting with the following questions. (Consult pages 2435–2436 of the *ESV Study Bible* for further insights; also available online at esv.org.)

1. God Is Love (4:7–12)

John is adamant: it is impossible to know God but not love others. He uses strong words to make his point inescapable (compare vv. 19–21). Which expressions in this paragraph do you find most convicting concerning the absolute necessity for Christians to love? Why are they so convicting?

In 3:9–10, John used the image of children inheriting the likeness of their parents. How does John return to the same analogy in this passage concerning love (4:7–8)?

Twice, in short succession, John describes Christ's atonement for our sins as the chief display of God's love for us (vv. 9–10). Compare these parallel descriptions and note one or two emphases unique to each of them.

a. "In this the love of God was made manifest . . ." (v. 9):

b. "In this is love . . ." (v. 10):

In many pagan[1] religions, worshipers show love for their gods by adorning the deities' visible images (idols) with food, clothing, or other gifts. How does the Christian's inability to see God redirect us in where we look for his image as we express our love for him (v. 12; compare vv. 19–21; Gen. 1:27; James 1:27)?

2. We Love Because He First Loved Us (4:13–21)

John repeats many of the same themes from the previous paragraph (vv. 7–12) in this second paragraph (vv. 13–21). List the repeated phrases and ideas that you notice.

Between the statements "by this we know" (v. 13) and "so we have come to know" (v. 16), John describes a role each person of the Trinity fulfills in our salvation. How does the Trinitarian character of salvation demonstrate the fundamental place of love in our faith (vv. 13–16)?

God's love is revealed in our initial salvation (vv. 13–16) and continues to perfect us "for the day of judgment" (vv. 17–18). How does the certainty of God's love provide confidence to anticipate eagerly—and not to fear—the final judgment?

Read through the following three sections on *Gospel Glimpses, Whole-Bible Connections,* and *Theological Soundings.* Then take time to consider the *Personal Implications* these sections may have for you.

Gospel Glimpses

THE FATHER'S INITIATIVE. John's words in verse 9 echo those of Jesus in his conversation with Nicodemus: "God so loved the world, that he gave his only Son, that whoever believes in him should not perish but have eternal life" (John 3:16). It is not our love for God that stirs him to take notice of our plight, hear our cries, or respond with provision for our deliverance. The Bible points to God the Father as the author and sole initiator of our salvation: "In this is love, not that we have loved God but that he loved us and sent his Son to be the propitiation for our sins" (1 John 4:10).

SALVATION BY FAITH. The apostles present eyewitness testimony of God's great love made manifest to us in Christ Jesus. It is they who "have seen and testify that the Father has sent his Son to be the Savior of the world" (1 John 4:14). Exposing unbelievers to the testimony of the apostles in the Gospels is an essential feature of any ministry of evangelism.[2] Whenever someone, upon hearing that testimony, "confesses that Jesus is the Son of God, God abides in him, and he in God" (v. 15). By faith alone, anyone who hears and believes the witness of the apostles concerning Jesus is restored to communion with God.

Whole-Bible Connections

ONE ANOTHER. John is writing to Christians as he repeatedly instructs them to "love one another." This is a theme we find repeated throughout the New Testament: Christians are especially called to love fellow believers (Rom. 12:9–13; 1 Cor. 12:12–25; Eph. 4:25–32). This is not to avoid the duty to love nonbelievers as well (Gal. 6:10). In fact, it is often harder to love other Christians (from whom we expect greater Christlikeness) than to love nonbelievers, just as children in a family sometimes find it easier to get along with friends than with siblings. Nevertheless, Jesus declares that love among Christians for one another is our most powerful witness to the unbelieving world: "A new commandment I give to you, that you love one another.... By this all people will know that you are my disciples, if you have love for one another" (John 13:34–35). We could say that John actually *participates* in this message in his repeated exhortations for Christians to "love one another."

IMAGE OF GOD. The Old Testament temple was unique among the temples of the ancient world. Other nations had idols enthroned in the inner sanctums of their temples. Israel's temple was also a house for its God, with a throne room in the inner sanctum. But the throne room of Israel's temple had no image of God in it. In fact, it did not even have a throne, only a "footstool" (the ark was designed as a "footstool"; Pss. 99:5; 132:7). Other nations mocked Israel for having no image of God in its temple (Ps. 115:2–8), but God was not to be represented by man-made images (Deut. 4:15–31; 5:8–10). Nevertheless, God has not left the world without a likeness of himself. Genesis 1:26–27 uses the same Hebrew word (*tselem*) commonly identified with idols as "images" of a deity to identify humans as the "image" of God. Sin has corrupted that likeness (Rom. 3:9–18) but has not erased it. John picks up on that scriptural theme of humanity as the image of God in order to urge us to show our love for God by our care for his "images" all around us (1 John 4:12; compare vv. 19–21).

Theological Soundings

WORSHIP. Christians often think of worship services as gatherings in which we may show our love for God. While we do confess our love for God in worship, the real significance of worship is that God shows his love to *us*. Worship is when God invites us into his house. Through his Word and sacraments, God refreshes us in his great love for us. We are then to respond and show our love for God, principally as we go out of worship services and back into our communities. It is by our deeds of care for one another that we respond to God's great love (James 1:27).

LOVE. John declares that "love is from God" and "God is love" (1 John 4:7–8). There is no higher ideal of love by which God could be measured; God himself is the source and ideal of love. All love that exists anywhere in creation is the fingerprint of God, who is himself love by nature and the source of all love in creation. The church father Augustine argued that this so because God is triune, and therefore his very nature is one of perfect social communion: love.

Personal Implications

In this week's passage, John presses home the central exhortation of his epistle: to cease from love for the world and instead to love the Father (2:15–17). And we show our love for the Father by loving one another. Make notes below on some personal implications for your walk with the Lord under the three headings we have considered and on the passage as a whole.

1. Gospel Glimpses

2. Whole-Bible Connections

3. Theological Soundings

4. 1 John 4:7–21

> ## As You Finish This Unit . . .

Psalm 133 is a short psalm that captures the spirit of John's exhortations in this week's passage. Read aloud or sing that Psalm, then pray for God's grace to "love one another" as you grow in your gratitude for God's great love for you.

Definitions

[1] **Paganism** – Any belief system that does not acknowledge the God of the Bible as the one true God. Atheism, polytheism, pantheism, animism, and humanism, as well as numerous other religious systems, can all be classified as forms of paganism.

[2] **Evangelism** – Proclamation of the gospel (Greek *euangelion*) of Jesus Christ.

WEEK 7: CHILDREN OF GOD

1 John 5:1–12

The Place of the Passage

This passage constitutes the final lesson in the main body of John's epistle. Here John presents the final arguments for the two major themes of his message: the priority of accepting by faith that Jesus is the Son of God, whereby we become children of God; and the necessity of love for our brothers and sisters in the church. These are the lessons John has been developing throughout the epistle, as he encourages us to overcome the sins of the world and to grow in our love for God.

The Big Picture

Faith in Christ makes us children of God who cease from loving the world as we grow in love for one another.

Reflection and Discussion

This passage is separated into two readings below. Read the first portion, pausing to answer the questions provided for it, before interacting with the second

portion. (Additional information on the passage is available in the *ESV Study Bible*, page 2436, or at esv.org.)

---

1. Faith and Love (5:1–5)

What is the basis for our being "born of God," and what is the fruit that follows in those who are indeed born of God (vv. 1, 4)? These two answers summarize the heart of John's message.

John knows that we sin (2:1), struggle to love as we ought, and need this exhortation he is writing to us (2:7–11). Why, then, does John write so absolutely, even saying things that leave no exception, such as, "*Everyone* who loves the Father loves whoever has been born of him" (5:1)?

John has written extensively in this epistle about "loving one another." But genuine love is more than a warm feeling. What does genuine love actually look like? Where does John point us for guidance in godly love (vv. 2–3; compare Gal. 5:14)?

John's message emphasizes our calling to love, yet he continues to exalt faith as the power behind the Christian life. What does it mean to "overcome the world" by faith (1 John 5:4–5; compare 2:15–17)?

2. Faith and Life (5:6–12)

John points to the Spirit as the one who gives testimony about Jesus, by two signs: "the water and the blood" (v. 6). The "water" likely refers to Jesus' baptism, at the beginning of his public ministry. How did the Spirit bear witness to Jesus in his baptism (see John 1:32–34)?

The "blood" likely refers to the crucifixion, at the end of Jesus' ministry. How did the Spirit bear witness to Jesus through the crucifixion (see John 20:1–31)?

Humans bear witness with words, but the Spirit bore witness to Jesus with signs (John 20:30–31). What specifically do these two signs (the water and the blood; 1 John 5:6) certify concerning Jesus (vv. 9–10)? And what does faith in these signs certify concerning those who believe in Jesus (vv. 10–12)?

Reread the "proposition statement" at the beginning of John's epistle (2:15–17). How does this passage at the culmination of the epistle (5:1–12) develop the ideas of that opening exhortation?

Read through the following three sections on *Gospel Glimpses*, *Whole-Bible Connections*, and *Theological Soundings*. Then take time to consider the *Personal Implications* these sections may have for you.

► Gospel Glimpses

BORN OF GOD. This epistle is full of the gospel![1] One of the most important gospel images that John has woven throughout the letter is the promise of a new birth. In 2:29 John introduced the imagery of being "born of him." There he led us to marvel at the nature of such love, "that we should be called children of God" (3:1). Throughout the epistle, this notion of being "born of God" has provided the backbone for the resulting duty to "love one another" as brothers and sisters created in God's image. It is this concept of new birth that binds together our love for the Father and our love for one another as two sides of the same new status granted us through faith. This gospel theme running throughout the letter is brought to a climax in this week's passage: "Everyone who believes that Jesus is the Christ has been born of God" (5:1).

THE CROSS. John places special emphasis on the shedding of Christ's blood as an event wherein the Spirit testified to Jesus. "This is he who came by water and blood—Jesus Christ; not by the water only but by the water and the blood" (v. 6). Earlier in the letter, John pointed to the sacrifice of Jesus for our sins as the greatest demonstration of love (3:16–17; 4:9–10). That same marvel emerges in this week's passage, as John pauses to emphasize the particular significance of "the blood" among the signs whereby the Spirit testifies to us that Jesus is the Son of God.

Whole-Bible Connections

GOD'S COMMANDMENTS. Throughout the New Testament, Jesus and the apostles tell us that the Old Testament law teaches us to love (Matt. 22:34–40; Mark 12:28–34; Luke 10:25–28; Rom. 13:8, 10; Gal. 5:14). John picks up on that same principle in his exhortation to love God and love one another by "obey[ing] his commandments" (1 John 5:2). As a system of laws for Old Testament Israel, these commandments could be regarded as burdensome. But as lessons on love, John urges us to understand that "his commandments are not burdensome" (v. 3). It is faith, after all, not the law, that gives us victory over the world (v. 4). We are not saved by law; nevertheless, we learn to love from the law. Jesus satisfied the perfect holiness required in the Old Testament law (Matt. 5:17) and also fulfilled the works of redemption signified by the law's rituals[2] (Heb. 4:14–16; 10:5–10). The Old Testament rituals are no longer to be practiced (Gal. 5:1–6; Rom. 10:4), but our study of the Old Testament ceremonies continues to teach us about the atonement Jesus completed (Heb. 9:1–28). Likewise, the Ten Commandments, accompanied by the various judicial and moral laws of the Pentateuch,[3] continue to show us what righteousness looks like. Thus, for example, in 1 Corinthians 9:8–12 Paul quotes a statute from the Mosaic law about the care of oxen as embodying a principle from which the New Testament church derives guidance on the fair pay of her ministering leaders.

TESTIMONY. In the Old Testament, the testimony of a witness required corroboration. A single witness would not suffice, but "only on the evidence of two witnesses or of three witnesses" was a matter to be confirmed (Deut. 19:15). John draws on this principle in his identification of two testimonies to Jesus ("the water and the blood"; 1 John 5:6)—indeed, he actually mentions "three that testify: the Spirit and the water and the blood; and these three agree" (v. 7–8).

Theological Soundings

SON OF GOD. John uses two titles of Jesus interchangeably in this passage. On the one hand, he calls us to believe "that Jesus is the Christ" (1 John 5:1). On the other hand, he calls us to believe "that Jesus is the Son of God" (v. 5). Both of these related terms draw from titles of Old Testament kingship. In Psalm 2, for example, each successive heir to David's throne is called to be God's "Anointed" (Ps. 2:2; "Anointed" is the English translation of the Hebrew title "Messiah," which also translates as "Christ" in Greek) and also a "Son" of God (Ps. 2:7; compare 2 Sam. 7:14). Both of these titles reflect the particular duty of the Davidic king to embody God's Spirit (hence the notion of anointing) and likeness (hence the notion of sonship) among the people. David and his subsequent heirs could never perfectly satisfy this high calling until Jesus arrived, who, as testified by the Spirit in his baptism ("the water") and resurrection ("the blood"), was pleasing to the Father as the perfect Christ and the true Son of God.

SACRAMENTS. John identifies "three that testify" (1 John 5:7) to the fact "that Jesus is the Son of God" (v. 5). More specifically, there is One Person who testifies ("the Spirit is the one who testifies"; v. 6), and that Person provides his witness through two signs ("by water and the blood"; v. 6). These signs likely refer to the baptism and crucifixion of Jesus, which marked the beginning and the end of his public ministry. They also marked two points at which the Spirit of God miraculously confirmed Jesus as our representative sacrifice (John 1:32–34; 20:1–31). These are also the two aspects of Jesus' identification with us in which the Christian participates, through baptism and communion. It is likely that John uses the sacramentally significant terms "water and blood" to identify the Spirit's signs specifically in a manner that draws the believer's thoughts to the sacraments of baptism and the Lord's Table.

▶ Personal Implications

The promises extended to those who believe are amazing! Do you believe that Jesus is the Christ? Reflect on the various encouragements for your faith in this passage. As you do, write down your reflections under the three headings we have considered and on the passage as a whole.

1. Gospel Glimpses

2. Whole-Bible Connections

3. Theological Soundings

_____

_____

_____

_____

_____

_____

4. 1 John 5:1–12

_____

_____

_____

_____

_____

_____

▶ As You Finish This Unit . . .

Read the passage again, this time reading it with the insight of your study in mind. Consider any further insights that you discover as you read it yet again, and devote yourself to prayer to praise God for his grace and to seek his Spirit's help to grow in your faith.

Definitions

[1] **Gospel** – A common translation for a Greek word meaning "good news," that is, the good news of Jesus Christ and the salvation he made possible by his crucifixion, burial, and resurrection. "Gospel" with an initial capital letter refers to each of the biblical accounts of Jesus' life on earth (Matthew, Mark, Luke, and John).

[2] **Ritual** – A symbolic action performed for religious purposes.

[3] **Pentateuch** – The first five books of the Bible.

WEEK 8: THAT YOU MAY KNOW

1 John 5:13–21

The Place of the Passage

We now come to the end of John's first epistle. Typically, speeches and sermons in New Testament times began with an introduction (called the *exordium* in the rhetoric of the time) and main exhortation (*propositio*), which is then developed by a series of proofs or arguments (*probatio*) forming the speech's body, and finally is capped with a rousing conclusion (*peroratio*). This week's passage is John's *peroratio*, wherein he wraps up his message with a concise series of conclusions. The phrase "we know" or "that you may know" is repeated seven times as John sums up the doctrines he desires his readers to embrace. The main conclusion is stated up front: "I write these things . . . that you may know that you have eternal life" (1 John 5:13). But this "eternal life" about which John writes is not just a future hope. It is a present, dynamic relationship with the Father. It is present growth in victory over sin. It is the present experience of newness of life. John draws all of these glorious truths into this closing paragraph and seals it with a final plea summing up our proper response to the gift of eternal life: "Little children, keep yourselves from idols" (v. 21).

> ## The Big Picture

Considering the eternal life we have received from God, we must not love the world or the things of the world (which is idolatry).

> ## Reflection and Discussion

If time allows, reread the entire first epistle of John, including the closing passage now at hand. Reviewing the whole epistle will help you pick up on the various threads John ties together in this conclusion. At minimum, read this week's passage carefully before responding to the reflection prompts below. (Avail yourself of the study notes on this passage in the *ESV Study Bible*, page 2437, and online at esv.org.)

1. Confidence in Prayer (5:13–17)

John draws one main conclusion up front: "I write these things ... that you may know that you have eternal life" (1 John 5:13; compare v. 20; John 20:30–31). In light of the opening paragraph of the epistle (1 John 1:1–4), what does John have in mind when he refers to "eternal life"?

How does the topic of prayer (5:14–17) offer an ideal focal point for our participation, even now, in the gift of eternal life? How do the epistle's themes of love for God, love for one another, and victory over sin all find practical expression in the Christian privilege of prayer?

In verse 14, John states that God answers prayers that are "according to his will." In verses 16–17, John elaborates on one implication of this parameter for prayer: it requires that we pray for others according to the terms of the gospel. We should pray for victory over sin on behalf of "a *brother* [i.e., a fellow Christian] committing a sin." But we cannot pray for victory over sin on behalf of one who rejects Christ. (The "sin that leads to death" likely refers to those who abandon Christ; compare 2:18–25.) We must, of course, pray for unbelievers to repent and come to Christ (1 Tim. 2:1–6). But we cannot expect God to grant them the fruits of new life until they do repent (1 John 5:4). Thus to pray "according to his will" here means to pray in keeping with the terms of the gospel. What does John's discussion teach concerning the topics that ought to be central to our prayers?

2. Three Things We Know (5:18–20)

The letter closes with three resolutions, each introduced by the statement "We know . . ." (vv. 18, 19, 20). These three convictions undergird our confidence that we have eternal life through Christ (v. 13). Summarize in your own words the three conclusions anchoring John's message of eternal life:

a. verse 18:

b. verse 19:

c. verse 20:

John paints a vivid picture of temptation: "he who *has been* born of God" (a Christian) is protected by "he who *was* born of God" (Jesus) from "the evil one"

(v. 18; compare 5:4–5). How should this description of a personal Savior and a personal enemy impact our perception of temptation and conviction?

The title "son" is often used for someone who represents another, much as a son would represent his father in business negotiations in the world of the Bible. How does John describe the significance of this title for Jesus (v. 20)? Why is it so exciting to recognize that the man Jesus is the "Son of God"?

3. Keep Yourselves from Idols (5:21)

John's first epistle ends with a one-line exhortation: "Little children, keep your-selves from idols" (v. 21). Reread the epistle's opening exhortation in 2:15–17 and discuss how this final command summarizes that exhortation.

By definition, an "idol" serves as a focal point for expressing one's love for the deity it represents. Where are the children of God to look for God's "image" in order to show our love for him (see 4:12, 20; Gen. 1:27)?

Read through the following three sections on *Gospel Glimpses*, *Whole-Bible Connections*, and *Theological Soundings*. Then take time to consider the *Personal Implications* these sections may have for you.

Gospel Glimpses

SON OF GOD. In 1 John 5:20, John identifies two aspects of Jesus' mediation. First, he "has given us understanding, so that we may know him who is true." Jesus mediates God's likeness to us (see 1:2, 5). Second, Jesus mediates our restoration to communion with God: "We are in him who is true, in his Son Jesus Christ" (5:20). Jesus not only mediates God "down" to us but also mediates our relationship "up" to him (see 1:3, 6–7). Thus John closes his depiction of Jesus under these two titles: "He is the true God [the manifestation of God to us] *and* eternal life [the one who brings us into communion with God]."

Whole-Bible Connections

IDOLS. The book of Numbers describes the final stage of Israel's exodus[1] from Egypt, recounting their journey from Sinai to the border of the Promised Land. God had done great wonders in Egypt to break the yoke of slavery and free Israel from Pharaoh's oppression. God had given Israel his laws at Mount Sinai, forming them into a kingdom for his own possession. He had provided for them through 40 years of wandering in the wilderness. Notwithstanding these great mercies of God, Numbers recounts what happened the first time Israel encountered the Canaanite god Baal: "Israel yoked himself to Baal of Peor" (Num. 25:3). Throughout the Bible, God's mercies have been answered by faithlessness and idolatry.[2] Nevertheless, God continues in his patient work of forgiveness to restore us to himself through Christ. In this epistle, John contributes to this whole-Bible theme of God's forgiveness and repeats the exhortation stressed throughout the Bible: "Little children, keep yourselves from idols" (1 John 5:21).

THE EVIL ONE. From the first pages of Genesis, human sin is presented as a betrayal of God by means of man's placing his trust in the lies of the Devil[3] instead of trusting God's word. In our modern secular age, Christians are eager to defend the reality of a good God but we often neglect the reality of the Evil One who seeks to "steal and kill and destroy" (John 10:10). But John reminds us that sin is both a betrayal against Christ and also a surrender to "the evil one" (1 John 5:18). Keeping this personal face on the battle with sin is an important theme throughout the Bible.

Theological Soundings

PRAYER. It is noteworthy that John chooses the topic of prayer as the climactic demonstration of God's love for us and our love for one another (1 John 5:14–17). A common response when one sees a brother or sister committing sin is to gossip. But notice the response that John teaches us: "If anyone sees his brother committing a sin . . . , he shall ask [God] . . ." (v. 16). As Christians, our duty is to pray for one another in our struggles with sin. We are also encouraged to "ask anything" in prayer (v. 14). The expansive terms "ask anything" and "whatever we ask" (v. 15) are not intended to suggest a shopping-spree approach to prayer, however. Rather, these phrases are here to assure us that no area of our lives is too small for or irrelevant to the love of God for us. We are to bring all our burdens and petitions to him. And we do so with great confidence because we know that, however foolish or ill-advised our petitions might be, God will always answer them in keeping with his own good, generous, and wise purposes.

Personal Implications

As you reflect on these closing verses of 1 John, make notes below on some personal implications for your walk with the Lord under the three headings we have considered and on the passage as a whole.

1. Gospel Glimpses

2. Whole-Bible Connections

3. Theological Soundings

----

4. 1 John 5:13–21

▶ As You Finish This Unit . . .

Take advantage of the gift of prayer, backed by the promise of eternal life and its fruits for God's people, as taught by John in this week's passage. Pray for yourself and for one another to grow in your love for Christ and hatred for sin. Also review the three "we know" declarations in 1 John 5:18–20, and turn those into three topics to pray about in thanksgiving and confession of faith before God.

Definitions

[1] **The exodus** – The departure of the people of Israel from Egypt and their journey to Mount Sinai under Moses' leadership (Exodus 1–19; Numbers 33). The exodus demonstrated God's power and providence for his people, who had been enslaved by the Egyptians. The annual festival of Passover commemorates God's final plague upon the Egyptians, resulting in Israel's release from Egypt.

[2] **Idolatry** – In the Bible, idolatry usually refers to the worship of a physical object. Paul's comments in Colossians 3:5, however, suggest that idolatry can include covetousness, since it is essentially equivalent to worshiping material things.

[3] **The Devil (Satan)** – A spiritual being whose name means "accuser." As the leader of all the demonic forces, he opposes God's rule and seeks to harm God's people and accuse them of wrongdoing. His power, however, is confined to the bounds that God has set for him, and one day he will be destroyed along with all his demons (Matt. 25:41; Rev. 20:10).

WEEK 9: COVER LETTER TO THE CONGREGATION, PART 1

2 John 1–6

▲

The Place of the Passage

All three epistles of John were probably sent together as a single packet (see "Overview"). Second John is probably a cover letter to the congregation introducing the written sermon that we studied the past several weeks (1 John). As a cover letter, this brief epistle identifies the sender, addresses the recipients, and offers a synopsis of key points in the attached sermon. The cover letter motivates the congregation to give full attention to the main sermon, and its study should help us to take fully to heart what we have learned in our study of 1 John. In the first half of the cover letter (2 John 1–6), John introduces the positive exhortation to "[walk] in the truth" (v. 4). Next week's portion will introduce the negative warning to "watch yourselves" (v. 8) and avoid false teachings.

The Big Picture

Jesus is the Christ who leads us into true obedience to God's commandments by teaching us to love.

Reflection and Discussion

Read the entire epistle. We will look at only the first half this week, but read the whole letter and then use the following questions to reflect on the first six verses. (See page 2441 of the *ESV Study Bible* for additional helps; online at esv.org.)

1. Salutation (vv. 1–3)

John loves to use vivid images. He identifies himself as "the elder" and addresses the church as "the elect lady and her children" (v. 1). At the end of the letter, he will further identify his own congregation as "the children of your elect sister" (v. 13). Jot down your thoughts on the meaning of each of these terms and on how each helps us understand the relational character of the church.

Typically in the ancient world, religions were defined by ethnicity. But Jesus extends his church "throughout the whole world . . . to all nations" (Matt. 24:14). If race and language are not what unifies citizens of Christ's kingdom, then what is the bond that unites us (2 John 1–2)?

John's greeting of "grace, mercy, and peace" (v. 3) matches similar greetings in other New Testament epistles. The normal salutation in letters of that time was the word "Greetings!" (Gk. *chairein*; literally, "joy to you"). Complete the following chart, filling in the boxes for the salutations used in each of the New Testament epistles. Then discuss the significance of the way in which New Testament Christians said "hello" in correspondence.

Rom. 1:7			Titus 1:4	
1 Cor. 1:3			Philem. 3	
2 Cor. 1:2			Hebrews	(No salutation.)
Gal. 1:3			James 1:1	
Eph. 1:2			1 Pet. 1:2	
Phil. 1:2			2 Pet. 1:2	
Col. 1:2			1 John	(No salutation.)
1 Thess. 1:1			2 John 3	
2 Thess. 1:2			3 John	(No salutation.)
1 Tim. 1:2			Jude 2	
2 Tim. 1:2			Rev. 1:4	

The word "truth" appears four times in this short salutation, and in two of those occurrences it is coupled with "love." What is John indicating, even in the letter's salutation, about the relationship between truth and love?

2. Walk in Truth and Love (vv. 4–6)

"Some of your children" (some of the congregants) continue "walking in the truth" (v. 4). This "some" is probably in contrast with those who recently abandoned the faith (v. 7; 1 John 2:18–19). The remnant's faithfulness causes John to "rejoice greatly." But confessing the truth is not enough. What further exhortation does John introduce in this cover letter (2 John 5) that he develops more fully in the main epistle (1 John)?

John asserts that the commandments Israel had "from the beginning" were given to teach love (vv. 5–6; compare 1 John 5:2–3; Gal. 5:14). Read the Ten Commandments (Ex. 20:1–17) and write some notes as you consider how these commandments teach us to love.

John uses the image of "walking" three times in this passage (2 John 4–6). Why do you suppose he writes of "walking in the truth" rather than of "speaking the truth"?

Read through the following three sections on *Gospel Glimpses*, *Whole-Bible Connections*, and *Theological Soundings*. Then take time to consider the *Personal Implications* these sections may have for you.

Gospel Glimpses

ELECT LADY. John identifies the receiving congregation as the "elect lady" (2 John 1; compare v. 13). The biblical term "elect"[1] means "called out" or "chosen."

It is a term of love, reminding God's people that they were chosen by him: "we love because he first loved us" (1 John 4:19; compare 1 Cor. 1:26–28). Furthermore, the English translation "lady" accurately captures John's Greek term of nobility. He addresses the church as an "elect lady [*kuria*]," using the title of a lord's (*kurios*) wife. The church is the bride of *the* Lord, chosen in love by him.

TRUTH. John repeats the word "truth" four times in his salutation. Each time, he uses the term to refer to the gospel. John loves the congregation to whom he writes "in truth" (2 John 1). Other Christians are identified as "all who know the truth" (v. 1). We are those who not only know the truth but also have "the truth that abides in us ... forever" (v. 2). Furthermore, we anticipate the "grace, mercy, and peace" of God to be at work among us through "truth and love" (v. 3). The doctrines of God's grace are trustworthy and true and are therefore suitably described as "truth."

> ## Whole-Bible Connections

GRACE, MERCY, PEACE. Nearly all of the New Testament epistles open with variations on the common theme of "grace, mercy, and peace" from God. Of all of the New Testament epistles, only James uses the conventional salutation of "Greetings!" "Grace" is the cornerstone that begins almost every New Testament salutation. *Grace* is the favor God holds toward us, which is the basis for his deeds of *mercy* that result in the restoration of *peace* between him and his people. In this simple salutation in its varied forms, nearly every New Testament epistle opens with a succinct gospel declaration.

COMMANDMENTS. The significance of the commandments God gave his people on Mount Sinai is captured in the song of Moses in Deuteronomy 33:1–5: "The LORD came from Sinai. ... Yes, he loved his people, ... so they followed in your steps, receiving direction from you, when Moses commanded us a law, as a possession for the assembly of Jacob. Thus the LORD became king in Jeshurun." Israel had gone down into Egypt as a household (Gen. 46:8–27), but God multiplied them in Egypt and brought them to Mount Sinai to constitute them as a kingdom, with himself as their King. His commandments were given as a "covenant"[2] (Deut. 5:2), defining the nature of that kingdom as a society of love centered in his gift of atonement. John picks up on this Old Testament theme and points to the gospel as fulfilling the community of love that the commandments had foreshadowed (2 John 5–6).

BRIDE. John identifies the congregation to which he writes as the "elect lady" (2 John 1), with the Greek word for "lady" indicating the bride of a lord (see "Elect Lady" above), and his own congregation as an "elect sister" (v. 13). This imagery continues an Old Testament pattern for describing the various communities of faith. In the Old Testament, the city of Jerusalem was regarded as the "bride" of the Lord (Jer. 2:2; compare Rev. 21:2) and all of the other towns and villages as "the daughters of Judah" (Pss. 48:11; 97:8). Through these images, the whole nation was regarded as a network of households bound together under the same marriage covenant with the Lord. John uses similar metaphors to describe the churches as a family united to Christ by marriage.

Theological Soundings

FOREVER. Throughout his epistles, John speaks of the eternality of God's love using terms like "abide" (26 times), "eternal" (6 times), and "forever" (2 times). The present order of the world, in its brokenness and sin, might seem hopelessly permanent. But "the world is passing away along with its desires" (1 John 2:17). John seeks to shake us free from the false idea that the present state of things is permanent. He points to what truly is abiding and immutable: the truth of God's great love, and the inheritance he has granted to us in Christ. We rejoice "because of the truth that abides in us and will be with us forever" (2 John 2).

Personal Implications

John exhorts us not merely to "know the truth" (2 John 1) but also to "[walk] in the truth" (vv. 4, 6). Make notes below on some personal implications for your walk with the Lord under the three headings we have considered and on the passage as a whole.

1. Gospel Glimpses

2. Whole-Bible Connections

3. Theological Soundings

_____
_____
_____
_____
_____

4. 2 John 1–6

_____
_____
_____
_____
_____

▶ As You Finish This Unit . . .

It is difficult to read any part of John's letters without being overwhelmed at the love of God. Clearly, John was overwhelmed at the greatness of God's love, and he endeavors in every line to stir in us the same sense of wonder. Give thanks to God for his love as you have been stirred to reflect upon it anew, and pray for his help as you minister his love to others.

Definitions

[1] **Election** – In theology, God's sovereign choice of people for redemption and eternal life. Also referred to as "predestination."

[2] **Covenant** – A binding agreement between two parties, typically involving a formal statement of their relationship, a list of stipulations and obligations for both parties, a list of witnesses to the agreement, and a list of curses for unfaithfulness and blessings for faithfulness to the agreement. The OT is more properly understood as the old covenant, meaning the agreement established between God and his people prior to the coming of Jesus Christ and the establishment of the new covenant (NT).

WEEK 10: COVER LETTER TO THE CONGREGATION, PART 2

2 John 7–13

The Place of the Passage

The previous portion of John's cover letter to the congregation introduced the call to "[walk] in the truth" as taught by the apostles. But there are false teachers who seek to draw us away from the truth about Christ. The church to which John wrote had recently lost many of its members to such "antichrist" teachers (1 John 2:18–19). Therefore, the second half of John's cover letter introduces the importance of learning to recognize and guard against such false teachers. Altogether, this short cover letter serves to stir the congregation to the vital importance of the doctrines taught in full in John's written sermon (1 John).

The Big Picture

We must reject as false those whose teaching does not stand in line with that of the apostles.

> **Reflection and Discussion**

Reread last week's passage as well as this week's text. Use the questions below to help you consider the second half of the epistle. (See the *ESV Study Bible*, pages 2441–2442, for additional helps; online at esv.org.)

1. Watch Out for False Teachers (vv. 7–11)

Some theologians believe there will be a single, final "antichrist" who will deceive the whole world at the end of time. That teaching is based on different New Testament passages than these, since John uses the term "antichrist" to refer to many false teachers throughout history. What qualifies a person to bear the title "antichrist" in John's warnings (v. 7; compare 1 John 2:18–19, 22; 4:2–3)?

Scholars debate the identity of the "deceivers" in 2 John 7. Does John refer to "those who do not confess [the *fact of*] the coming of Jesus Christ in the flesh" or to "those who do not confess [the *teachings about*] the coming of Jesus Christ in the flesh"? Under the first interpretation, the false teachers are those who deny that Jesus was fully human. In later centuries, a heresy did emerge called *docetism*, which taught that Jesus was a spirit being and not incarnate. But it is doubtful that John's audience faced that particular heresy. The second interpretation is more likely, especially in view of the subsequent exhortation to "abide in *the teaching* of Christ" (vv. 9–10). False teachers are those who reject the testimony about Jesus from those who knew him in the flesh (1 John 1:1–4). Where can we find the "teaching of Christ" that provides us with the authoritative standard by which we are to judge between true and false teachers? How do we know that it is true?

John was one of the last—and possibly the very last—of the apostles to die. Like wolves, many false teachers were already circling to snuff out the movement the apostles had worked hard to establish. Compare Paul's warning in Acts 20:28–32 with John's exhortation in 2 John 8–9. On what foundation did the apostles place their confidence for the church's survival after their departure?

John urges us to remain faithful in hope of a "full reward" (v. 8). What does John identify, in verse 9, as the substance of that reward?

John tells us not to learn from false teachers (vv. 8–9), nor to materially support them (vv. 10–11). In John's day, itinerant teachers depended on the housing and financial support of local residents in places where they traveled to teach. What are contemporary ways in which false teachers seek support from Christians?

2. Final Greetings (vv. 12–13)

John has repeatedly emphasized the importance of truth that bears the fruit of love. How does John's longing to teach his audience in person, rather than communicating only by letter, illustrate the proper character of the church (v. 12; compare Rom. 1:11; 1 Thess. 2:17–19; 3:6; 2 Tim. 1:4)? Does this have implications for the importance of gathered worship and face-to-face Bible study in an age of online social networks? If so, how?

Read through the following three sections on *Gospel Glimpses*, *Whole-Bible Connections*, and *Theological Soundings*. Then take time to consider the *Personal Implications* these sections may have for you.

Gospel Glimpses

THE FOUR GOSPELS. In 2 John 7, John gives a significant "title" for the apostolic confession concerning Christ's earthly ministry. He is likely referring to the whole history of Christ's life and work, as witnessed and recorded by the apostles in the four Gospels. We generally call these four testimonies of the apostles "the Gospels" (i.e., Matthew, Mark, Luke, and John). John gives another title for that body of testimony concerning the life and works of Jesus, calling it "the coming of Jesus Christ in the flesh." This title is probably drawn from the prologue of his own Gospel, in which John introduces his biography of Jesus as "the Word" who "became flesh and dwelt among us" (John 1:1, 14). Faith in the gospel is trust not simply in God's promises but in God's sending Jesus to fulfill those promises in the flesh.

ABIDING IN GOD. In 2 John 9, John reminds us how important it is for Christians to know and believe the apostles' testimony concerning Jesus. He equates the one who "abide[s] in the teaching of Christ" with the one who "has both the Father and the Son" (v. 9). It is through faith in the life and ministry of Jesus that we are established in communion with God.

Whole-Bible Connections

FACE TO FACE. The apostles fulfilled their ministry primarily through in-person preaching, teaching, exhorting, and compassion. It is to our benefit that they also undertook to write down the messages they proclaimed and the acts that they performed. But the work of the church should never be reduced to a mere transfer of information through lectures or writing. Jesus is assembling a community of faith. The New Testament writers, including John, frequently express their longing for "face to face" fellowship (v. 12; 3 John 14; compare Rom. 1:11; 15:23; Phil. 1:8; 1 Thess. 2:17–19; 3:6; 2 Tim. 1:4; 4:9).

ANTICHRISTS. The apostles wrote four Gospels (Matthew, Mark, Luke, and John), further supplemented with epistles, the book of Acts, and Revelation. These writings enable the church in all ages to "confess the coming of Jesus Christ in the flesh" with the apostles (v. 7; compare 1 John 1:1–4). It is the work of Jesus that fulfills the community of love promised in the Old Testament commandments (2 John 4–6; compare 1 John 5:1–5). But there were those in the synagogues and the temple in New Testament times who denied that Jesus was the Christ. Mostly Pharisees, Jewish scribes, and other temple leaders, these opponents of the apostles taught that God's people were to fulfill the commandments of God and thus restore communion with the Father apart from Jesus (v. 9; 1 John 2:23). John uniquely uses the title "antichrist" for these opponents, but the other New Testament writers also describe these same teachers (see John 5:18–47; Acts 4:17–18; 6:13–14; Rom. 2:17–3:26; 1 Cor. 1:22–24; Heb. 12:18–25; etc.)

Theological Soundings

HEAVENLY REWARD. Pop-culture notions of heaven frequently envision big, white mansions with other symbols of wealth and ease. But the biblical vision of heaven is of a different character altogether. John encourages us to anticipate our "full reward" in 2 John 8, which he defines in terms of relationship: "Whoever abides in the teaching has both the Father and the Son" (v. 9). The great inheritance we long to possess is not centered in "stuff" but is found in unhindered communion with God. To dwell in perfect fellowship with the Lord has implications for our health, our material possessions, and our overall welfare (Rev. 7:15–17; 21:1–4). But the focus of our heavenly reward is the renewal of fellowship with God (1 Pet. 1:3–9).

SCRIPTURE. The faith of God's people has always been rooted in written texts. Other religions of the ancient world were centered on idols and ritual divination.[1] But Israel had no idols (Deut. 4:15–31) and was forbidden from participating in divination (Deut. 18:9–14). Instead, the God of Israel revealed himself in words, spoken to his people and written down by prophets (Deut. 18:15–22). The apostle John takes up "paper and ink" (2 John 12) and participates in this pattern of writing down Scriptures for the authoritative guidance of God's people.

Personal Implications

John writes in order to help us grow, "that our joy may be complete" (v. 12). Make notes below on some personal implications for your walk with the Lord under the three headings we have considered and on the passage as a whole.

1. Gospel Glimpses

2. Whole-Bible Connections

3. Theological Soundings

4. 2 John 7–13

> ### As You Finish This Unit . . .

The body of this epistle begins and ends with words of joy (vv. 4, 12). Pick one of your favorite songs of praise to sing in order to stir your heart to rejoice in God's grace, and then close your study of this passage in prayer.

Definition

[1] **Divination** – The attempt to acquire special knowledge about the future or other naturally unknowable information by interpreting phenomena such as dreams, heavenly bodies, or animal intestines, or by the casting of lots. All divination is condemned in Deuteronomy 18:14.

WEEK 11: COVER LETTER TO THE PASTOR

3 John 1–15

> ### The Place of the Passage

This last of John's three epistles is probably his cover letter to the pastor, whose name is Gaius (3 John 1). John sets aside the vague generalities characterizing the congregational letters (1–2 John). In this letter to the pastor, John calls out by name an individual (Diotrephes; v. 9) who has been hindering good teachers in the church. John also tells Gaius that his courier, Demetrius (v. 12), is carrying a letter that is to be read to the congregation (v. 9). This is probably a reference to the written sermon (1 John), bundled with these cover letters. In his letters to the congregation (1–2 John), John wrote in general terms about efforts to undermine the church's access to the apostolic witness. In this private letter to Gaius, we find that this threat is real. Pastor Gaius will need to ensure that Diotrephes fails in any effort to stop John's courier from presenting his message to the gathered church. This short cover letter to the pastor completes the picture begun in John's other two letters.

The Big Picture

The church must be protected from error by putting a stop to false teachers, and the church must be enriched in the apostolic witness by promoting the labors of faithful preachers instead.

Reflection and Discussion

John's third letter can be outlined based on the three individuals John mentions (see the "Outline" of 3 John, in Week 1 of this study). Read the entire epistle and then reflect on each section and each personality introduced by John. (Helpful insights are available in the *ESV Study Bible* on pages 2445–2446; online at esv.org.)

1. Beloved Gaius (vv. 1–8)

John speaks of Gaius as one of his "children" (v. 4), whose perseverance[1] in the truth brings the apostle great joy. What expressions of John in his introductory address to Gaius draw out the deep love between these two men of God (vv. 1–4)?

The church where John is located has apparently sent missionaries to the city where Gaius pastors, using the city as a launching point to new frontiers among the Gentiles. (On the possible identity of these two cities, refer back to "Date and Historical Background," in Week 1.) John commends Gaius for his hospitality and support for these missionaries and comments on the testimony these missionaries have brought back to John concerning Gaius's love (vv. 5–8). In what ways do you or your church continue this pattern of supporting missionaries who are seeking to reach new frontiers?

Compare John's warning in 2 John 10–11 to his commendation in 3 John 8. How do these mirroring statements instruct us concerning the importance of cautious yet generous giving?

2. Wicked Diotrephes (vv. 9–10)

Diotrephes is evidently a person of influence within the church that Gaius pastors. Perhaps he is another pastor in the church or a wealthy member who hosts the church in his home (see Acts 16:14–15). Whatever his role, he has the ability to receive people into, or block them from, the church at large. Gaius must intervene to ensure that Diotrephes fails to block Demetrius from delivering the accompanying letter to the congregation. What two sins does John identify as motivating Diotrephes in his troublemaking (3 John 9)?

Elsewhere, John mentions his desire to visit the congregation face-to-face to rejoice with them in the truths of the gospel (2 John 12; 3 John 14). What else does John intend to handle when he comes in person (v. 10)? What do these varied purposes teach us about the nature of pastoral ministry?

3. Faithful Demetrius (vv. 11–12)

John quotes a maxim in verse 11 both to encourage Gaius to welcome Demetrius and also to condemn Diotrephes for his lack of hospitality to the brethren.

Compare this saying in verse 11 to John's discussion of love in 1 John 4:7–8. What is John teaching us to expect to see in ourselves if we are in a living relationship with God?

John certifies Demetrius as a minister who has passed both his "character exam" ("received a good testimony from everyone") and his "theology exam" ("received a good testimony . . . from the truth itself"), with the added affirmation of the apostles (v. 12). In what ways can the examination process for church leaders today follow this same protocol?

4. Final Greetings (vv. 13–15)

John again states his preference for face-to-face ministry (3 John 13; compare 2 John 12). As modern-day readers of John's letters, we are blessed that he did send the letters before visiting in person. Nevertheless, John insists on waiting to address certain issues in person (3 John 10). How might John's example of discretion concerning what to do in writing and what to do in person (and, indeed, what to write to the congregation versus what to write to the pastor) challenge us in our prudent use of the many communications media available to us today?

In John's cover letter to the congregation (2 John), he used familial images to describe the relationships between congregations (2 John 1, 13). Here he uses the title "friends" to describe such relationships (3 John 15). What does it tell us about the nature of the church that John uses this term—not only within a given congregation but also between congregations?

Read through the following three sections on *Gospel Glimpses, Whole-Bible Connections,* and *Theological Soundings.* Then take time to consider the *Personal Implications* these sections may have for you.

Gospel Glimpses

DEMETRIUS. John sends his letters to Gaius's church by the hands of a minister named Demetrius. The name of this faithful preacher is itself a testimony of God's grace. Demetrius's name means "devoted to Demeter," who was the Greek goddess of crops and harvests. Therefore Demetrius was not a name that Jewish or Christian parents were likely to give to a son at birth, and therefore this Demetrius was almost certainly a Gentile man born into a pagan household. Yet Jesus redeemed this man who had been devoted to Demeter at birth, transforming him into a faithful minister of the gospel.

Whole-Bible Connections

HERALDS. Demetrius joins a list of apostolic couriers mentioned in the various New Testament epistles. Paul sent many of his epistles by a preacher named Tychicus (Eph. 6:21–22; Col. 4:7–9; compare Titus 3:12). He sent his epistle to the Romans by the hand of "our sister Phoebe, a servant of the church at Cenchreae" (Rom. 16:1). Peter's associate named Silvanus delivered letters for him (1 Pet. 5:12). John apparently sent his bundle of letters in the care of Demetrius (3 John 12). Several of these couriers are specifically charged to explain the letters upon their delivery (Eph. 6:22; Col. 4:8). In other words, the apostolic epistles were typically intended to be preached upon delivery.

FREE GOSPEL. Itinerant teachers were common in the Roman Empire. Such traveling speakers typically collected fees or contributions for their speeches. The apostles, however, were determined that the gospel would always be presented free of charge. Therefore, the apostles either worked to earn their own living when on the road or else went with support from their sending churches (Acts 18:2–5; 1 Cor. 9:3–18). John supports this principle in 3 John 5–8, urging Gaius's church to support the missionaries heading into new frontiers so that they could preach the gospel while "accepting nothing from the Gentiles" in return.

Theological Soundings

APOSTOLIC CHURCH. In the Nicene Creed, we confess our faith in the "one holy catholic and apostolic church." Even though the church is physically separated into various geographical locations, and even when the church is divided into theological factions, there is ultimately only one bride of Christ. And the defining bond of that church is the writings of the apostles (the New Testament Scriptures). Even in the days of the apostles, there were others who sought to provide the church a different foundation. Diotrephes (vv. 9–10) is an example, since he "does not acknowledge our [the apostles'] authority" (v. 9) but seeks to alienate messengers from the apostles, such as Demetrius (v. 10), in order to reshape the church after his own version of Jesus. Paul had warned that the church's greatest danger would be not attack from outside but rather false teachers "from among your own selves" who defy the apostles (Acts 20:29–30). One of the reasons the apostles left their teachings in written form was to ensure that the church would be able to guard against these false gospels and remain true to the message of Christ as faithfully preserved by his apostles (1 John 1:3–4; 2 John 8).

PRIDE. Diotrephes resisted the apostles because of his own desire to be pre-eminent:[2] "Diotrephes . . . likes to put himself first" (3 John 9). This reminds us that the church is not about personalities and celebrity but about promoting the name of Christ Jesus alone.

HEALTH. John's primary concern is with the spiritual health of Gaius and the church he pastors. Nevertheless, while John has received word about Gaius's spiritual vigor (v. 3), he has received no news of Gaius's physical health. John therefore prays for Gaius's physical health also (v. 2), reminding us that the church should be concerned about both physical and spiritual well-being.

Personal Implications

What lessons from John's third epistle had the greatest impact on you? Make notes below on some personal implications for your walk with the Lord under the three headings we have considered and on the passage as a whole.

1. Gospel Glimpses

2. Whole-Bible Connections

3. Theological Soundings

4. 3 John 1–15

As You Finish This Unit . . .

Think about the pastors who have faithfully ministered the Gospel to you through the years, and give thanks to God for them. Pray for the physical well-being as well as the spiritual growth of your pastor(s). Consider what false teachings are currently distracting many Christians in this day, and pray for the church's protection and nurture in the faith of the prophets and apostles.

Definitions

[1] **Perseverance of the saints** – God's enabling all true believers to remain faithful to the end. Those who willfully continue in sin reveal that they were never truly believers. Others may for a time appear to abandon their faith though they have not in fact done so. This doctrine does not deny the reality that even true believers still sin, nor does it mean that those who have made a profession of faith are free to live sinful, godless lives.

[2] **Preeminence** – The quality of being first, foremost, or of highest significance. In the Bible, this quality is attributed supremely to Christ (Col. 1:18).

WEEK 12: SUMMARY AND CONCLUSION

▲

As we finish our study of John's epistles, we will reflect on these books' over-arching message and themes. After that, questions will be posed concerning the various *Gospel Glimpses*, *Whole-Bible Connections*, and *Theological Soundings* encountered throughout the course of our study of these letters.

The Big Picture of 1–3 John

The early church father Jerome recorded a story he had received concerning the apostle John. Jerome lived nearly three centuries after John, so the historicity of the story is dubious. But it suitably captures the spirit of John's epistles nevertheless. According to Jerome, when John grew too old and frail to preach, his attendants would carry him to the worship assembly. And even though he could not preach, he would give this single exhortation, over and over: "Little children, love one another." One day, a young man in the congregation urged John to tell them something new, instead of repeating himself so much. But John is said to have replied, "It is the Lord's command, and if this is all you do, it is enough."

Jerome's story is probably just a legend. But, like many legends, it is designed to preserve a lesson. We do not know what the aged John might have said in person in the assembly in Ephesus. But in his epistles, the elderly apostle wrote in words that do seem repetitive: "Love one another." Yet John wrote this message with such earnestness because it is the message he had heard from the Lord himself.

Other themes John has woven through the letter include *sin* ("I am writing these things to you so that you may not sin"; 1 John 2:1); *obedience to God's commandments* ("This is the love of God, that we keep his commandments. And his commandments are not burdensome"; 1 John 5:3); *truth* ("I have no greater joy than to hear that my children are walking in the truth"; 3 John 4); *eternal life* ("I write these things . . . that you may know that you have eternal life"; 1 John 5:13); and the *apostolic witness* ("That which we have seen and heard we proclaim also to you"; 1 John 1:3). But all of these themes ultimately feed into that practical exhortation to love one another.

John defines sin as loving the world, and the opposite of sin is to love God and one another. The purpose of God's commandments is to teach us what it means to love God and love one another. The Spirit of truth and the witness of the apostles concerning Christ teach us to abide in him and to love one another. The fruit of eternal life is victory over sin and love for one another.

It may be too reductionistic to say that John's epistles are exclusively about Christian love. Nevertheless, the varied landscapes of themes and truths described in these letters find a common thread in the expectation that Christians, reborn as children of God, will reflect his likeness in separation from the lusts of the world and in love for one another.

Read through the following three sections on *Gospel Glimpses*, *Whole-Bible Connections*, and *Theological Soundings*. Then take time to consider the *Personal Implications* these sections may have for you.

Gospel Glimpses

The epistles of John are saturated with the gospel. He ends his written sermon (1 John) the same way he concludes his biography of Christ (the Gospel of John). John's Gospel ends, "These are written so that you may believe that Jesus is the Christ, the Son of God, and that by believing you may have life in his name" (John 20:31). Similarly, 1 John ends, "I write these things to you who believe in the name of the Son of God, that you may know that you have eternal life" (1 John 5:13).

Review the various "Gospel Glimpses" from this study. Which of these perspectives into the gospel did you find particularly refreshing, insightful, or otherwise edifying? Why?

In our study of 1 John, we identified 1 John 2:15–17 as the main exhortation of the epistle (compare 1 John 5:21). How does this main exhortation relate to the gospel hope of eternal life and to its fruits of love?

▶ Whole-Bible Connections

If all the books of the Bible were placed along a timeline from beginning to end, the epistles of John would be close to the end of the line. John was among the last survivors of the generation of the apostles. Consequently, these epistles pick up many themes and promises traced through the rest of the Bible and provide a final rousing exhortation to believe and walk in this great heritage. John literally begins with Genesis (his many "from the beginning" citations early in 1 John), takes us through the commandments of God, and follows the line of biblical hope to Jesus as received in the church ("fellowship") of the apostles.

Review the various "Whole-Bible Connections" throughout the course of this study. Which of these broader themes of Scripture did you find particularly refreshing, insightful, or otherwise edifying? Why?

Many Christians find John's positive characterization of God's commandments to be surprising. What conclusions have you drawn from the way John, writing in the light of the gospel, repeatedly references the Old Testament commandments (see 1 John 2:3–4; 3:22–24; 5:2–3; 2 John 6; compare 1 John 3:4)?

The word *love* appears more often in the epistles of John than in any other book of the Bible except the Psalms. But John certainly does not have exclusive claim to that important theme! What other books or passages of the Bible do you consider as contributing to the message of love developed by John?

Theological Soundings

The apostle Paul is typically considered the preeminent theologian of the New Testament church. But John's epistles are by no means lacking in theological rigor. John tends to write in practical, pastoral terms. Nevertheless, his reasoning is constructed around careful, rich doctrinal realities. Review the various "Theological Soundings" from this whole study. Which of these doctrinal topics identified in John's epistles did you find particularly refreshing, insightful, or otherwise edifying? Why?

In addition to the theological topics identified in each passage, were there other points of theology or insights into the truths and ways of God that stood out to you through the course of this study? If so, what were they?

If love is the leading exhortation emerging from John's epistles, what are two or three other important beliefs or truths John develops in these letters?

Personal Implications

God has given us his Word to transform us. What are one or two ways in which these weeks of close study of the epistles of John have challenged or changed you?

What are the implications of 1–3 John for your prayers and for the church's efforts in evangelism?

What implications should we draw from the epistles of John for our participation in the fellowship and worship of the church?

As You Finish Studying 1–3 John . . .

We rejoice with you as you finish studying the epistles of John! May this study become part of your Christian walk of faith, day by day and week by week throughout all your life. Now we would greatly encourage you to study the Word of God on a week-by-week basis. To continue your study of the Bible, we would encourage you to consider other books in the *Knowing the Bible* series, and to visit www.knowingthebibleseries.org.

Lastly, take a moment to look back through this study. Review the notes that you have written, and the things that you have highlighted or underlined. Reflect again on the key themes that the Lord has been teaching you about himself and about his Word. May these things become a treasure for you throughout your life—this we pray in the name of the Father and the Son and the Holy Spirit. Amen.

KNOWING THE BIBLE STUDY GUIDE SERIES

Experience the *Grace* of God in the *Word* of God, Book by Book

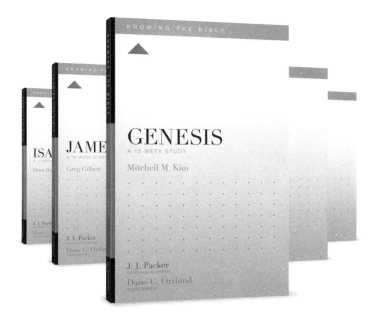

GENESIS

A 12-WEEK STUDY

Mitchell M. Kim

J. I. Packer

Dane C. Ortlund

--- **Series Volumes** ---

- Genesis
- Exodus
- Leviticus
- Numbers
- Deuteronomy
- Joshua
- Judges
- Ruth and Esther
- 1–2 Samuel
- 1–2 Kings
- 1–2 Chronicles
- Ezra and Nehemiah
- Job
- Psalms
- Proverbs
- Ecclesiastes
- Song of Solomon

- Isaiah
- Jeremiah
- Lamentations, Habakkuk, and Zephaniah
- Ezekiel
- Daniel
- Hosea
- Joel, Amos, and Obadiah
- Jonah, Micah, and Nahum
- Haggai, Zechariah, and Malachi
- Matthew
- Mark
- Luke

- John
- Acts
- Romans
- 1 Corinthians
- 2 Corinthians
- Galatians
- Ephesians
- Philippians
- Colossians and Philemon
- 1–2 Thessalonians
- 1–2 Timothy and Titus
- Hebrews
- James
- 1–2 Peter and Jude
- 1–3 John
- Revelation

crossway.org/knowingthebible